LEVI'S TASTES OF AMERICA

AMERICA ,A MELTING POT OF PEOPLE AND FOOD

I DEDICATE THIS TO THE LOVING MEMORY OF MY DEAR MOTHER AND GRANDMOTHER. IT IS BECAUSE OF THEM I HAVE THE PASSION FOR FOOD AND THE DESIRE TO INSURE THAT FOODS FROM OUR MOTHERS, GRANDMOTHERS, AND GREAT GRANDMOTHERS ARE PASSED TO FUTURE GENERATIONS TO ENJOY AND CREATE THEIR OWN MEMORIES OF GREAT FOOD AND GREAT TIMES TOGETHER.

IN AN ERA OF FROZEN, BOXED, HOME DELIVERED AND TAKE OUT THESE RECIPES MAY ALL BUT BE FORGOTTEN. AS A SINGLE PARENT A LOT OF THESE RECIPES I OUT OF SHEER NECESSITY LEARNED AND AM NOW PASSING ON TO A GENERATION OF FAST FOOD JUNKIS HOPING THAT IT MAY HELP ENCOURAGE THEM TO RETURN TO THE "OLD SCHOOL" WAY OF ENJOYING A GREAT MEAL "HOME COOKED" .

HERE IS A COMPILATION OF RECIPES ,SOME FROM VERY EARLY IN OUR COUNTRIES HISTORY SOME FROM WITH IN THE LAST 100 YEARS OR SO. THEY COME FROM THE MANY PEOPLES AND CULTURES BEING BROUGHT HERE OVER SEA'S AND LAND.SOME MAY SEEM COMPLICATED SOME ON THE EASY SIDE DEPENDING ON YOUR OWN COOKING SKILLS. . BE ADVENTUROUS AND TREAT FRIENDS AND FAMILY AND YOURSELF OF COURSE TO A DELIGHTFUL MEAL. REMEMBER SOME OF THESES RECIPES ARE ALL BUT FORGOTTEN SO ENJOY EACH MEAL AND SHOW OTHERS WHAT THEY ARE MISSING.

* As my 2 idols Albert Einstein and Martha Stewart have said "Simple, But not to simple"*

SECTIONS:

MY PERSONAL FAVORITE MUST HAVE RECIPES

SALADS AND STARTERS

ENTREES'

SIDE DISH'S

MY PERSONAL FAVORITES AND MUST HAVE RECIPES

TEXAS STEAK SANDWICH

PREP. 30

Cook: 15

SERVES: 6 SANDWICHS

LEVEL: EASY

INGREDIENTS:

* 6 crusty rolls such as Portuguese or country sourdough, split lengthwise .

* 1/3 cup Dijon mustard

* 1 1/2 pounds grilled steak medium rare, preferably porter house, rib eye or

hanger thinly sliced

* Kosher salt

* Fresh cracked pepper.

* 3/4 pounds Maytag Blue cheese cut in 12 slices

* 1 to 2 red onions sautéed.

* 1 head Butter lettuce (cleaned)

Directions:

Pre-heat broiler to 400 degrees.

Toast the rolls split side up under broiler until golden brown.

Transfer rolls to work area and slather with Dijon mustard top with beef over lapping the meat. Season with salt and pepper. Cover each portion of the meat with blue cheese slices.

Place under broiler until the cheese is melted .Remove place on serving plates and top with red onions and butter lettuce. Serve immediately.

Tasty luncheon or dinner served with a crisp salad. If you do not care for blue cheese replace with Swiss or aged cheddar.

* My friend asked to fix me lunch one afternoon and asked if I liked Blue cheese. I said it was my least favorite but I would try what ever he made. Since that day Blue cheese has become my favorite above all. It is one of the most versatile tastes which I have found pairs well with many foods. Try it even if you are certain you hate it (blue cheese), you may change your mind.*

LEVI'S SPICY ZUCCHINI , PEPPER AND POTATO SOUP

Prep: 1 hour

Cook: 40 minutes

Serves: 4

Level: Easy

Ingredients:

* 1 large red bell pepper for roasting

* 3 tablespoons extra virgin olive oil

* 1 to 1 1/4 pounds zucchini thinly sliced into disks

* 2 Fresno chili's seeded and sliced into rings

* 2 mild green Cubanelle peppers sliced into rings

* 1 medium rd or yellow onion peeled and sliced into rings

* 3 to 6 baby Yukon gold potatoes' , very thinly sliced into disks

* 4 cloves garlic thinly sliced

* sea salt and freshly cracked black pepper

* 2 tablespoons freshly chopped rosemary

* A few sprigs of thyme picked and chopped fine.

* 2 pounds peeled heirloom tomatoes chopped OR 1 (28-ounce) can fire roasted or stewed tomatoes.

* 2 to 3 cups chicken or vegetable broth

* Fresh sweet basil leaves chopped for garnish

* crusty bread or baguette for serving

Directions:

Roast red and green peppers over open flame until charred . Set aside to cool. After cooling scrape all black from peppers and thinly slice .Heat 3 tablespoons extra virgin olive oil in Dutch oven over medium heat. When oil ripples add zucchini, peppers onions, potatoes and freshly chopped herbs salt and pepper and saute until tender. Add tomatoes and cook until tomatoes begin to break down. Stir in enough broth to your desired consistency. As thick or thin as you prefer.

Serve in shallow bowls with sweet basil and warmed buttered bread of your choice.

*A great way to warm up on a chilly fall afternoon or as a starter for a delightful winter evening meal. I came up with this recipe out of necessity one day when I discovered I had not much else to fix for lunch. It is now requested frequently by my family. I have refined the ingredients over the years to come up with what I write today. *

CHICKEN SEATTLE ALA LEVI

Prep: 20

Cook: 20

Serves: 4

Level: Easy

Ingredients:

* 2 pounds boneless chicken breasts

* 1 stick real butter salted

* 1 large cucumber peeled and seeded

* 1 can marinated artichoke hearts drained

* 1 pint heavy cream

* 1 lemon

Directions:

In butter and heavy cream slow cook chicken breast over low heat until completely done. Add cucumber and artichoke hearts drizzle with fresh lemon juice and serve.

Serve with fresh roasted veggies and rice pilaf for a lighter meal or over pasta of your choice for a heartier meal.

Do not over heat cucumbers and artichoke hearts as it will drastically change the flavor of this dish.

This recipe was something I had in the early 1980'S at my favorite Seattle restaurant and the Chef would not give me the exact recipe but, he said what he would give me was enough for me to figure it out on my own at home, and with a little trial and error I did. I love this dish and usually only share it with the most special people in my life outside of my own family.

MOM'S UNION CITY STEW

Prep: 30 minutes

Cook: 4 1/2 to 5 hours

Serves: 6

Level: Easy

Ingredients:

* 2 pounds cubed beef filet or rib eye.

* 1 pound carrots cut in 1 inch pieces

* 1 pound celery cut in 1 inch pieces

* 1 large white onion chopped into medium pieces

* 2 large green bell peppers cut into 1 inch pieces

* 5 to 6 potatoes washed, peeled and cut into 1 inch pieces (set aside in chilled water)

* 1 large 16 ounce and 1 small 12 ounce cans of whole tomatoes.

* 3 tablespoons instant tapioca

* 3 table spoons sugar

* salt and fresh cracked pepper

Directions:

Preheat oven to 300 degrees

In Dutch oven combine all ingredients (except potatoes) . Salt and pepper ,slightly toss cover and put in oven to bake 4 hours . DO NOT STIR WHILE BAKING. At last hour gently stir in potatoes and bake 1 more hour .

A delicious take on the everyday beef stew. Serve with homemade biscuits or sourdough rolls or even better Kentucky Spoon Bread and a garden salad. I believe Mom came across this recipe in the 1950's at a pot luck she attended in Indiana's farm country near Union City. Hence her calling it Union City Stew. It was one of my favorite dinners as a child and 50 plus years later is one of my kids, grand kids and friends favorite meals. Cooking has became the one biggest joys I have in my spare time . I was a single Dad for many years and for a time had minus zero extra time let alone spare to enjoy anything out side raising my kids and sometimes the friends they always drug home with them.

LEVI'S SOUTHERN FRIED CHICKEN GIZZARDS

Prep: 20

Cook: 8 minutes

Serves: 4 as entree 8 to 10 as a starter

Level: easy

Ingredients:

* 2 pounds cleaned chicken gizzards

* 1 cup corn meal

* 2 cups flour

* 4 eggs

* 1 pint half and half

* 3 tablespoons Lawry's seasoned salt

Directions;

Boil chicken gizzards 20 minutes and drain . Cool to touch for next step.

PREHEAT DEEP FRYER TO 375 DEGREES

Combines corn meal flour and 2 tablespoons Lawry's seasoned salt and divide into 2 flat bowls. In another bowl beat eggs and 1/4 cup half and half .

Next to deep fryer set up bread area as follows 1 bowl corn meal /flour mixture , next 1 bowl egg wash and last another bowl of breading mixture. Dip cooled gizzards into flour then egg wash and again in flour mixture and

drop into deep fry until golden and crispy.(apprx. 3 to 4 minutes) Drain and lightly salt with Lawry's seasoned salt.

Serve immediately with your choice of sides or as a starter for any southern meal.

CHICKEN AND ASPARAGUS CREPES

Prep: 10 minutes

Cook; 20 minutes

Serves: 4

Level: Easy

Ingredients:

* 2 Tablespoons real unsalted butter

* 1 can cream of mushroom soup

* 1/2 small yellow onion chopped medium

* 1/8 cup dry sherry

* 1/4 cup shredded Fontina cheese

* 1 cup cooked chicken

* 8 white or green asparagus spears steamed till tender

* Savory crepes (recipe to follow)

* 1/2 shredded Swiss cheese

Directions:

Preheat oven to 350 degrees f. Lightly grease 13 inch by 9 inch baking dish.

In a large skillet melt butter over medium heat. Add cream of mushroom soup and onion and cook for 2 minutes. Stir in sherry, Fontina cheese and chicken . Cook until cheese has melted.

Spoon 1/4 cup chicken mixture down center of each crepe . Place 2 asparagus spears over chicken mixture. Fold in edges and roll each one up. Place seam side down in baking dish. Sprinkle 1/2 cup Swiss cheese over the top of crepes. Bake 10 minutes or until cheese is melted and crepes are hot.

Great as a light lunch or one of many delicious dish's on your luncheon buffet. Or for a delicious breakfast fair replace chicken with Canadian bacon and bake a s usual.

SAVORY CREPES

Prep: 8 minutes

Cook: 2 minutes

Serves 12 to 16 crepes

Level: Easy

Ingredients:

* 3/4 cups all purpose flour

* 1/2 teaspoon salt

* 1 1/4 cups whole milk

* 1 large egg

* 1 egg yolk

* 1 tablespoon melted butter

Directions:

In medium bowl mix flour and salt. In another bowl Whisk together milk and eggs and egg yolk. Gradually add flour to egg mixture until well blended.

Cook as per manufacturers directions. These may vary per manufacturer.

HERB AND GARLIC ROAST PORK

WITH HONEY MUSTARD SAUCE

Prep: 30 minutes

Cook: 1 hour

Serves: 4 to 6

Level: intermediate

Ingredients:

* 1 1/2 pound boneless pork loin

* Kosher salt and freshly cracked pepper

* 2 tablespoons extra virgin olive oil

* 2 tablespoons unsalted butter

* 1 tablespoon freshly chopped thyme

* 1 tablespoon freshly chopped flat leaf parsley

* 1 tablespoon freshly chopped rosemary

* 1 clove garlic minced fine

* 1 cup panko (Japanese bread crumbs)

* 1/3 cup plus 2 tablespoons Dijon mustard

* 2 whole heads garlic

* 2 tablespoons good quality honey

Directions:

Preheat oven to 375 degrees f. Sprinkle pork loin with salt and pepper. Heat a large oven proof skillet over medium high heat. Add the oil and pork loin and cook turning occasionally until brown on all sides . Transfer the pork to a cutting board.

Return the skillet to medium heat. Add the fresh herbs and cook about 1 minute. Stir in the panko and salt cook stirring until the panko is golden about 2 minutes. Transfer bread crumb mixture to waxed or parchment paper .

Brush the pork loin with 2 tablespoons mustard and roll in bread crumbs until well coated. Halve the garlic heads crosswise and add to the skillet with pork loin and roast until an instant read thermometer reads 145 degrees f. About 45 minutes .

Transfer the pork to a cutting board and let stand about 10 to 15 minutes allowing juices to redistribute in the meat.

Mean while, while pork loin stands place the skillet over medium low heat . Add the honey and remaining 1/3 cup Dijon mustard and stir until well combined. simmer until slightly thickened. About 2 minutes.

Slice the pork loin and serve with the roasted garlic and honey mustard sauce.

Pairs well with roasted root vegetables and rice pilaf. Finish off with a delectable southern strawberry pie. Left over pork makes a delicious sandwich for lunch the next day. This is a delicious variation on the every day roasted pork loin.

LEVI'S PERFECT PIE CRUST

Prep: 20 minutes

Inactive: 30 minutes

Yields: 2 (8 inch) pie crusts

Level: Easy

Ingredients:

* 2 1/2 cups all purpose flour

* 1/4 teaspoon fine sea salt

* 3 tablespoons fine granulated white sugar

* 1/4 cup very cold vegetable shortening

* 12 tablespoons ice cold real unsalted butter cubed

* 1/4 to 1/2 cup ice water

Directions.

In a large bowl sift together the flour ,salt and sugar. Add the shortening and as you begin to coat it all up with the flour. Add the butter cubes and work in well with a pastry cutter. Work it quickly so the butter does not begin to soft. The dough will be crumbly with the consistency of corn meal .Add the ice water a little at a time until the mixture comes together. Bring the dough together in a ball . Wrap in plastic wrap and refrigerate.

Do not over work the dough as it will cause it to become tough and non-flaky. When ready to use roll on a cold surface (marble works best) Roll out into 10 to 11 inch disks, each will make a 9 inch crust.

For no bake fillings , fill shells with beans and bake till golden brown , cool and fill with your favorite fillings. For baked in fillings fill and bake as per filling instructions. Usually 30 minutes to 1 hour..

Never go wrong with this pie crust . Done per instructions it will be soft and flaky every time.

FRESH BERRIES WITH BALSAMIC DRIZZLE AND AMERETTO CREAM

Prep: 15 minutes

Serves: 4 to 6

level: Easy

Ingredients:

* 1 pint raspberries

* 1 pint blue berries or black berries

* 1/3 cup balsamic vinegar

* 1/2 cup sugar

* 1 cup mascarpone cheese

* 1//4 heavy whipping cream

* 2 tablespoons confectioners sugar

* 3 tablespoons toasted almonds

* 2 tablespoons quality amaretto

Directions:

In small sauce pan bring together balsamic vinegar and sugar. Bring to boil and reduce by half (syrupy consistency) about 2 minutes.

In a small bowl whip together heavy whipping cream, mascarpone cheese , sugar and amaretto. Whip until light and fluffy.

When ready to serve layer the berries, a small amount of cheese mixture filling the dish. On top put a generous dollop of amaretto cream cheese mixture and drizzle with balsamic reduction and top with toasted almonds and serve.

A delicious and light end to any meal or replace amaretto cream with honey yogurt for a refreshing snack or early morning starter. I as a young man managed a well known local establishment on the airport in town. I had some very special guests flying in just for dinner one evening and had been asked to come up with a fresh berry dish to finish the meal. I spent the afternoon trying several combinations and this is the dish I served later that evening. These and other guests from that evening flew in many times over the years insisting they finish dinner with this. I hope you too enjoy it as many have.

SOUTHERN SWEET TEA

Total time 20 to 25 minutes

Ingredients;

* 6 iced tea sized tea bags

* 1 to 1 3/4 cups sugar

* 2 quart refrigerator iced tea container filled with ice

Directions:

In tea kettle boil iced tea bags in full kettle of water about 3 to 5 minutes until very dark in color. Mix in sugar to taste. Remove tea bags.

Pour sweetened tea over a full 4 quart pitcher of ice to chill and serve .

For a different taste add lemon wedge or fresh mint leaves stir and enjoy year round.

For a light cocktail add Italian Limoncello liquor and enjoy a refreshing summer cocktail by the pool .

Kentucky Spoon Bread

Prep: 10 minutes

Cook: 45 minutes

Serves: 6

Level: Intermediate

INGREDIENTS:

* 3 cups milk

* 1 ¼ cup cornmeal

* 1 tsp salt

* 1 3/4 tsp baking powder

* 3 eggs, whites and yolks separated

* 2 tablespoons butter

Directions:

Preheat oven to 350 degrees.

Lightly grease a 2 1/2 quart baking dish.

Separate the yolks and whites.

Heat 2 cups milk over medium heat just until bubbles start forming around the edge of the pan. We're only looking to scald the milk, not really boil.

Meanwhile, combine cornmeal, salt, and remaining 1 cup of milk. Whisk until smooth, then slowly add this cornmeal mixture to the hot milk. Cook and let come to a boil, then reduce heat and simmer for 5 minutes, stirring constantly.

Remove from heat then add the baking powder and butter, stirring to combine.

In the bowl with the egg yolks add 1/2 of hot cornmeal mixture to temper, fold in remaining of the hot cornmeal mixture gently. Tempering the yolks like this prevents them from cooking. Return the yolk mixture to the rest of the hot corn meal.

Beat the egg whites until stiff peaks form, then fold about 1/3 of the whites into the cornmeal mix. Once incorporated, fold in the rest until blended.

Transfer mix to the prepared baking dish and bake until puffed and golden brown, about 40 to 45 minutes. Serve warm.

Living in the south for many years as a child I was under the impression everyone knew of this type of cornbread. The recipe I use has been passed down since the early 1800's in my family. It is a soufflé type cornbread so remember keep the kids out of the kitchen and away from oven or it will fall just as any baked item with whipped egg whites. This is always served in my house with Union City Stew another old recipe from down on the farm. This takes patience and a lot of love to do correctly if your first try fails, try again until you get it right . It is worth the effort and your family will love you for it.

Friendly Monkey Bread

Prep: 30 minutes

Cook: 30 minutes

Serves: 10 to 12

Level: Easy

Ingredients:

* 3 (8 ounce) packages Pillsbury buttermilk biscuits

* 1 cup sugar

* 2 teaspoons cinnamon

* 1 cup butter (2 sticks)

* 1/2 cup packed brown sugar

Instructions:

Prepare Bunt pan by heavily greasing with butter. Preheat oven to 350 degrees F.

Cut each biscuit into four equal sized pieces.

Combine 1 cup sugar and 2 teaspoons cinnamon in a bowl or plastic bag. Drop roll the pieces of dough in the sugar cinnamon mixture and gently arrange them into the prepared Bunt pan.

In a small sauce pan, combine 1/2 cup of the remaining sugar cinnamon mixture with 1/2 cup brown sugar and 1 cup butter. Bring mixture just to a boil and then immediately remove from heat. Carefully drizzle the mixture over the rolled dough balls in the Bunt pan.

Preheat oven to 350 degrees.

Bake for 30 minutes. This time may vary depending on oven and pan used. Continue cooking until tops are starting to crisp and turn golden brown.

Allow pan to rest for about 10 minutes, then cover with a large plate and invert bread. To eat, pull desired amount off with your fingers and enjoy the gooey sweet sinful treat.

*This is a quick and easy way to serve a hot gooey treat on Sunday mornings with out spending hours in the kitchen. I used to get up at 5am have a cup of coffee and start making home made cinnamon rolls. One of my friends heard me telling my kids one Sunday morning to "appreciate my efforts and slow down and enjoy this early morning treat" (I

was a single Dad 40 years ago who also worked all week.).
All my desperate pleas fell on deaf ears I must admit as they
gobbled them down in seconds. The next day my friend came
by after work with 3 packs of store bought refrigerated
dough and this recipe. I have slept in until 9 am ever since on
Sundays. And now you should hear the cries of joy I get
from my Grand kids not to mention the " your the greatest
bestest Grandpa ever " It makes me warm and gooey inside .
Even gooier than these delicious treats. For a variations add
fresh blueberries or berries of your choice , so delicious.*

Sour Dough Bread Starter

Prep: 10 minutes

Inactive: weeks to months (if you feed and maintain the starter)

Serves: multiple loaves of fresh bread

Level: Intermediate

Ingredients:

* 1 (.25 ounce) package active dry yeast

* 2 cups warm water

* 2 cups all purpose flour

Directions:

In large glass bowl (GLASS ONLY), mix together dry yeast, 2 cups warm water, and 2 cups all purpose flour and cover loosely.

Leave in a warm place to ferment, 4 to 8 days. Depending on temperature and humidity of kitchen, times may vary. Place on cookie sheet in case of

When mixture is bubbly and has a pleasant sour smell, it is ready to use. If mixture has a pink, orange, or any other strange color tinge to it, THROW IT OUT! and start over. Keep it in the refrigerator, covered until ready to bake.

When you use starter to bake, always replace with equal amounts of a flour and water mixture with a pinch of sugar. So, if you remove 1 cup starter, replace with 1 cup water and 1 cup flour. Mix well and leave out on the counter until bubbly again, then refrigerate.

If a clear to light brown liquid has accumulated on top, don't worry, this is an alcohol base liquid that occurs with fermentation. Just stir this back into the starter, the alcohol bakes off and that wonderful sourdough flavor remains! Sourdough starters improve with age, they used to be passed down generation to generation!

*Even with a busy schedule this sour dough starter is well worth maintaining as it makes the best bread ever. I used to wonder why this smelly mixture was always around Granny's kitchen until after I became a single Dad and she added it to a gift basket of goodies with several recipes included. At that time a loaf of good sour dough bread at our local neighborhood bakery was about $2.69 (circa-1979-80). Not broke but always wanting to save a bit I tried one month to do the starter and make some bread and rolls with it. OH MY GOD why would any one ever buy store made sour dough bread or rolls again if they have this recipe on hand ? This

one is in her memory (Grandma Kathy) from me to you.
Enjoy and don't worry the effort is well worth it I promise.!*

Sourdough Bread

Prep: 4 1/2 hours

Cook: 35 to 40 minutes

Serves: 2 loaves or about 20 to 24 rolls

Level: Intermediate

Ingredients:

* 2 cups warm water

* 6 -8 cups flour (this depends on altitude and how thick your sourdough starter is)

* 1 cup sourdough starter

* 2 teaspoons salt

* 2 teaspoons sugar

* 1/2 cup cold water

* 1/2 teaspoon cornstarch

Directions:

In large mixing bowl add sourdough starter and stir in the salt and sugar and add flour 1/2 to 1 cup at a time to make a very stiff dough .

Knead till smooth.

Cover and let rise 2 to 2-1/2 hours.

Punch down and divide in half.

Knead till smooth and form into rounds. Place on a greased baking sheet. Cover lightly and let rise till double and puffy (1 to 1-2 hrs).

While this is rising mix the 1/2 cup water and 1/2 tsp cornstarch in a small bowl and microwave till boiling, remove from heat and let cool.

Preheat oven to 400 degrees.

Carefully place a small pan of hot water on the bottom rack of the oven.

Cut two slashes across each other on top of each loaf.

Bake for 10 minutes.

Pull out the rack and baste each loaf well with the cornstarch mixture.

Close the oven and allow to bake another 20-25 minutes. Loaves should be a light golden color and sound hollow when tapped on the bottom.

You are suppose to allow this to cool for 2 hrs to develop the sourdough flavor fully.

I suggest you do as I have learned over the years when I make the loaves, set one aside to completely cool, and the other dig into with in 30 minutes while it is still warm, slathering it with room temperature salted sweet cream real butter and enjoy the most delicious bread ever in my opinion. Instead of the 2 loaves divide the kneaded dough into little balls and proof as directed. For dinner rolls that are a compliment to any casual or formal occasion. I am still using sour dough starter from the original batch from the gift basket from Grandma in 1980's.

Cherry Delight

Prep: 30 minutes

Refrigerate: 2 to 4 hours

Serves: 8 to 10

Level: Easy

Ingredients:

* 1/2 cup graham cracker crumbs

* 2 tablespoons confectioners' sugar

* 2 tablespoons butter, melted

* 4 ounces cream cheese, softened

* 3/4 cup confectioners' sugar

* 1/2 cup whipped topping

* 1 (8 ounce) can cherry pie filling

Directions:

In a bowl, combine the graham cracker crumbs, confectioners' sugar and butter.

Press onto the bottom of an 8x4-in. loaf pan coated with cooking spray.

In a small bowl, using high speed on mixer whip cream cheese and confectioners' sugar until smooth; fold in whipped topping. Spread over crust. Spoon pie filling over top.

Refrigerate for 2 to 4 hours or until chilled.

*This dessert I can remember from a very young age at most family reunions, pot luck diners and even holidays. For a new twist use 1 (8 ounce can) raspberry pie filling instead . Either version is equally delicious. According to my Ohio friends this recipe dates from the 1920's or there about. I have been making it for 40 plus years and never get a complaint , that is unless I run out. *

SOUPS, SALADS AND STARTERS

Classic French Onion Soup

Prep; 30 minutes

Cook: 45

Serves: 4 to 6

Level: Easy

Ingredients:

* Sweet onions sliced thin

* 2 Large cloves garlic , minced

* !/3 cup good quality olive oil

* 2 tablespoons all purpose flour

* 8 cups beef stock

* 1/4 cup dry white wine

* 1/2 teaspoon fresh thyme minced fine

* 1 bay leaf

* 1 loaf day old French bread

* 2 cups Swiss cheese grated

* unsalted sweat cream butter

Directions:

Saute onion and garlic in oil over medium heat until tender and golden yellow. Sprinkle flour over onions and cook a few minutes more until flour turns golden colored . Add stock wine and bring to a boil. Add thyme

and bay leaf . Reduce heat and cook about 20 minutes .Salt and pepper to taste.

Mean while cut French bread 3/4 of and inch thick and butter each side. Toast until golden brown .Ladle soup into soup crocks , place 1 slice of toasted bread on each top with grated Swiss cheese and place under broiler until cheese is melted and golden brown.

Add a mixed green salad for a perfect winter lunch time warm up.

Shrimp and Andouille Gumbo

Prep: 30 minutes

Cook: 1 hour 30 minutes

Serves: 10

Level: intermediate

Ingredients;

* 1 red bell pepper , seeded and diced

* 1 green bell pepper , seeded and diced

* 2 large onions diced

* 2 celery stocks diced

* 3/4 cups vegetable oil (for more authentic taste use lard)

* 3/4 cups flour

* 2 bay leafs

* 1/2 tablespoon fresh cracked pepper

* 1/2 teaspoon cayenne pepper

  • 1/2 teaspoon ground white pepper*

  • 1/2 teaspoon dried thyme

- 1/2 teaspoon oregano

* 8 cloves minced garlic

* 5 1/2 cups shrimp stock (recipe follows)

* 1 pound andouille sausage cut into 1/2 inch pieces

* 2 pounds peeled shrimp (reserved from making stock)

* 10 servings cooked rice for serving

Directions:

Combine onions, celery, and peppers and have ready by stove in a separate bowl. In a large heavy skillet (preferably cast iron) heat 1/3 of oil just until it begins to smoke. Gradually add flour , whisking constantly. This step is most important for a true gumbo. Stir flour mixture constantly until completely cooked and has a dark brown almost burnt color and very fragrant. Add remaining oil and cook stirring with a wooden spoon for 2 minutes. Add salt and all dried spices and minced garlic and continue to cook another 2 minutes. Remove pan from heat.

Place shrimp stock in large cast iron Dutch oven or stock pot and bring to a gentle boil. Gradually add roux mixture to stock whisking constantly until well combined and totally dissolved . Add andouille sausage and sautéed vegetables reduce to simmer and cook 15 minutes. Add shrimp to pot and cook until shrimp is heated through. Salt and pepper to taste . If you prefer a spicy gumbo add a few red pepper flacks. Serve over s

Making a good roux can be tricky .For safety's sake wear oven mitts , use a good whisk and heavy cast iron skillet. Stir constantly at all times being sure bottom does not burn. If it does burn for the sake of a good gumbo start over . With practice you will be able to do this like a pro .

Your patience will be rewarded with a rich delicious gumbo.

Shrimp Stock

Ingredients:

* 2 pounds medium to large unpeeled shrimp

* 2 teaspoons vegetable oil

* 1 small onion cut in quarters

* 1 stock celery cut up

* 1 large carrot cut up 1/2 cup white wine

* 6 cups water

* 6 black pepper corns

* 1 bay leaf

* couple sprigs fresh thyme or 1/2 teaspoon died

Directions:

Peel and devein shrimp (reserve uncooked shrimp to add later to almost complete gumbo) In stock pot add all veggies and shrimp peels and wine. Cook until reduced by half . Add water bring to boil then reduce and cook over low heat 45 to 50 minutes. Occasionally skimming residue from top of water .Strain stock and reserve until you are ready to assemble gumbo.

* When love is used in preparation of this gumbo you will experience a true taste of the deep south and the Gulf Coast.

Shrimp and Okra Soup

Prep: 15 to 20 minutes

Cook: 10 to 15 minutes

Serves: 2

Level: Easy

Ingredients:

* 4 tablespoons Butter

* 1/3 cup finely chopped celery

* 1/3 cup finely chopped onions

* 1/3 cup finely chopped green pepper

* 1/4 cup roux (make roux in batches and keep a reserve on hand)

* 2 cups chicken or seafood stock

* 1 14.5 ounce can of okra with liquid

* 4 ounces tomato sauce

* 1/4 teaspoon garlic powder

* !/4 teaspoon thyme

* 1 bay leaf crumble into very tiny pieces

* 1/2 pound 60 count frozen shrimp

* 2 tablespoons chopped parsley

* 2 tablespoons chopped green onion

* 2 cups cooked rice for serving

Directions:

Melt butter in heavy 3 quart sauce pan and add all veggies and cook until translucent. Add roux and cook 2 to 3 minutes. Add remaining ingredients and simmer 3 to 4 minutes. Add shrimp and cook until shrimp begins to turn pink . Serve over rice.

* This is a fast version of a gumbo that is great for a luncheon served in a bread bowl or as a starter for a larger dinner party*

Pea Pesto Crustini

Prep: 10 minutes

Cook: 2 minutes

Serves: 4 to 6

Level: Easy

Ingredients:

* 1 10 ounce package frozen peas, thawed

* 1 clove garlic

* 1/2 cup fresh grated Parmesan

* 1 teaspoon kosher salt, plus extra for seasoning

* 1/4 teaspoon fresh ground black pepper, plus extra for seasoning

* 1/3 cup olive oil

* 8 to 10 slices baguette or ciabatta bread

* 1/3 cup olive oil

* 8 cherry tomato's halved for serving

For the pea pesto. Put together pea's , garlic and Parmesan, 1 teaspoon of salt and 1/4 teaspoon of pepper in food processor. Pulse until combined. With machine running slowly add olive oil until well combined , about 2 minutes. Season if need and set aside.

For the crustini, preheat stove top griddle , brush each slice of bread with olive oil and toast until golden brown and crusty on each side. . Transfer to serving platter and assemble using 1 to 2 teaspoons pesto on one side . Top with tomato halves and serve.

* If day old bread is not available place fresh cut slices in 300 degree oven and dry out *

Crab Salad in Endive Leaves

Prep: 20 minutes

Cook: 0

Serves: 6

Level: Easy

Ingredients:

* 4 tablespoon white wine vinegar

* 2 tablespoon Dijon mustard

* 1 teaspoon dried Oregano

* 1/4 teaspoon sea salt

* !/4 teaspoon fresh ground black pepper

* 2/3 cup extra virgin olive oil

* 24 ounces fresh crab meat (canned crab could be used but recommend fresh for best taste)

* 6 heads Belgian endive, cleaned and separated into spears

* Fresh chives chopped for garnish

Directions:

In a large bowl whisk together vinegar, mustard , oregano, salt and pepper until well blended. Add crab meat and stir to combine well.

Arrange endive on serving plates spoon crab mixture on each. Sprinkle with chives and serve .

* A must have at any dinner party . *

Crab Salad Napoleons with Fresh Pasta

Prep: 30 minutes

Cook: 10 minutes

Serves: 6

Level: Intermediate

Ingredients:

* 12 ounces fresh pasta sheets

* 1 cup Best Foods Mayonnaise (plus extra for pasta sheets)

* 1/2 cup fresh chives chopped fine (reserve 1/2 for garnish)

* 1 tablespoon fresh lemon juice

* 1/4 teaspoon fresh cracked pepper

* 1 pound lump crab meat (use best quality your market offers)

* 1 cup frozen peas , thawed

* 1 lemon zested for garnish

Directions:

Bring large pot of water to boil over high heat. Then add pasta and cook until tender. (Andante meaning tender but firm to bite) Drain under cold water to stop cooking process. Cut into 4 inch squares , each napoleon requires 3 squares.

In a large bowl combine mayonnaise , crab, pepper, lemon juice, crab meat and frozen peas and mix well.

To assemble spread Mayonnaise on pasta piece, top with about 1/4 cup crab salad , repeat 3 times . Garnish with pinch of lemon zest and chives and a bit of fresh cracked pepper .

Great starter for a small luncheon or served on your best china for a special dinner for your family and friends

Cioppino (Seafood Stew)

Prep: 30 minutes

Cook: 1 hour

Serves: 6

Level: Easy

Ingredients:

* 3 tablespoons olive oil

* 1 large fennel bulb , sliced thin

* 1 onion chopped

* 3 large shallots chopped

* 2 teaspoons sea salt

* 4 large garlic cloves finely chopped

* 3/4 teaspoon dried red pepper flakes

* 1/4 cup tomato paste

* 1 (28 ounce can) diced tomatoes in juice

* 1 1/2 cups dry white wine

* 5 cups fish or seafood stock

* 1 bay leaf

* 1 pound Manila clams

* 1 pound mussels , scrubbed and debearded

* 1 pound large shrimp peeled and deveined

* 1 1/2 pounds firm white fish (halibut is a great choice) cut in to 2 inch pieces

Directions:

Heat the oil over medium heat in a very large pot. Add the onions, shallots, and salt and sauté until onion is translucent, about 10 minutes. Add the garlic and 3/4 teaspoon of red pepper flakes, and sauté 2 minutes. Stir in the tomato paste then add the tomatoes and juice , wine. and fish stock and bay leaf. Cover and bring to a simmer. Reduce the heat to med-low. Cover and simmer until the flavors blend. about 30 minutes.

Add the clams and mussels. Cover and cook until the clams and mussels open. About 5 minutes . Add the fish and shrimp gently , simmer 5 minutes , just until both are cooked through. Stirring gently as to not break fish apart. Remove any clams and mussels that do not open. Season to taste with salt and pepper and add more red pepper flakes if desired. Serve immediately.

- This delicious stew can also be served any day with fresh bread for a delightful luncheon item*

•

East Coast White Clam Chowder

Prep: 20 minutes

Cook: 40 minutes

Serves: 6 to 8

Level: Easy

Ingredients:

* 1/2 pound real unsalted butter

* 1 Spanish (red) onion diced small

* 1/2 half pound all purpose flour

* 1 quart water

* 1 (55 ounce) can of clams

* 1/4 pound clam base

* 2 pounds peeled potatoes diced

* 1 pint half and half

Directions:

In a heavy pot melt butter and sauté onions until they become translucent. Add the flour and cook about 2 minutes making a very light colored roux. Add the clams, clam base and water stir to combine well. Add the potatoes and reduce heat and simmer until potatoes are tender. Add Half and half to taste. Garnish with chives and serve

*A very hearty and creamy taste of Americas east coast. Serve with crab cakes for a perfect luncheon. Serve this in a sour dough bread bowl for a perfect presentation at any meal. The first time i served this in bread bowls my kids felt it a must to caution every guest that "Dad's gone off the deep end , he thinks he can use bread for bowls." *

-

Crab Cakes

Prep: 30 to 40 minutes

Cook: 20 minutes

Serves: 4 to 6

Level: Easy

Ingredients:

* 1 pound good quality crab meat (free of an shells)

* 1/3 cup crushed oyster crackers

* 3 green onions finely chopped

* 1/2 cup green pepper finely chopped

* 1/4 cup mayonnaise

* 1 egg

* 1 teaspoon Worcestershire sauce

* 1 teaspoon dry mustard

* 1/2 lemon juiced

* 1/4 teaspoon garlic powder

* 1 teaspoon sea salt

* 1/8 teaspoon cayenne pepper

* 1 cup flour for dusting

* 1/2 cup good quality peanut oil

* Home made tarter sauce for dipping

Directions:

In a large bowl combine all ingredients accept flour and peanut oil. Mix very well.

Heat oil in large heavy skillet over medium heat. Mean time form your crab cakes and set to side. When the oil is hot and ready place crab cakes in pan and cook until golden brown on each side, Serve immediately .

'

* Substitute lobster meat for crab for a more elegant taste. These are a great starter, luncheon item or side dish for a perfect surf and turf dinner*

Spicy Seafood Salad

Prep: 10 minutes

Cook: 0 minutes

Serves: 4

Level: Easy

Ingredients:

* 10 imitation crab sticks (available at your local markets frozen section)

* 1/2 pound cooked chopped shrimp

* 1/4 pound cooked, chopped butter clams

* 3 shallots chopped

* 1/2 cup mayonnaise

* 3 tablespoons Tobiko (flying fish caviar) (available in any Asian market)

* 1 tablespoon Siracha hot chili sauce or hot sauce from your region of America

* Kosher salt

* Finely chopped chives for garnish

Pull crab sticks into strands and chop coarsely. In large bowl combine all ingredients and stir well to combine. Serve on butter lettuce leafs after chilling salad until well chilled.

* This is a perfect luncheon item for our " Lady's that Lunch" across the country , or any luncheon buffet*

Italian Pasta Salad

Prep: 10 minutes

Cook: 10 Minutes

Serves: 6 to 8

Level: Easy

Ingredients:

* 1/2 teaspoon sea salt

* 1 pound bow tie pasta

* 1 cup balsamic vinegar dressing (your favorite from your local market)

* 1/4 cup mayonnaise

* 1 tablespoon sugar

* 2 cups cherry tomatoes, cut in half

* 1 (4 ounce) can sliced mushrooms drained

* 2/3 cup pitted kalamata olives

* 1/2 green pepper diced small

* 1/2 teaspoon fresh cracked black pepper

* Grated Parmesan cheese for garnish

Directions:

Bring a large pot of water to boil. Add pasta and cook until tender according to package directions.

While the pasta is cooking, in a small bowl, whisk together balsamic vinaigrette, mayonnaise and sugar.

Drain the pasta and allow to cool. Add all remaining ingredients and too to combine well. Add the dressing and toss gently. Sprinkle with cheese and serve chilled.

This is great salad to add to any lunch menu.

Spinach Salad With Dried Cranberries ,Walnuts and Pomegranate

Vinaigrette

Prep: 5 minutes

Cook: -----

Serves: 4

Level: Easy

Ingredients:

* 1/2 cup pomegranate juice

* 2 tablespoons white wine vinegar

* 2 tablespoons olive oil

* 2 teaspoons Dijon mustard

* Sea salt and fresh cracked pepper

* 2 cups baby spinach leaves

* 1/3 cup dried cranberries

* 1/3 chopped walnuts

Directions:

In small container combine pomegranate juice, vinegar, oil and mustard. Seal and shake till very well combined.

Place spinach on serving platter and sprinkle with cranberries and walnuts. Pour dressing over spinach and serve.

* For an even tastier salad candy walnuts first. To do this melt 1 cup of good quality butter and 2 cups dark brown sugar, cook until slightly thick then toss walnuts in mixture to coat. Allow to cool. Delicious !!!!!!!!!*

Spinach And Blue Cheese Salad with Sliced Apples and Spiced Caramelized Pecans

Prep: 45 minutes

Cook: 35 minutes

Serves: 4

Level: Easy

Ingredients:

* 1 apple chilled and sliced (reserve in lightly salted water)

* 1 small lemon juiced

* 1 small head radicchio , cut into chiffonade

* 5 ounces good quality blue cheese (crumbled)

* Kosher salt and fresh cracked pepper

* 1/2 cup House dressing (recipe to follow)

* 1 1/2 cups spiced pecans (recipe t follow)

Directions:

Cut apple into 1/4's removing stems and seeds.(set aside in salted water or sprinkle with lemon juice to retard apples from browning)

When ready to serve combine apple, spinach , pecans, blue cheese and radicchio lettuce. Season lightly with salt and pepper and add dressing and toss. Divide into 4 equal servings and serve .

This is another dish where Bleu cheese becomes a surprising delight you will remember for future dinner parties and special occasions through out the year.

House Dressing

Prep: 15 minutes

Yield: 1 1/4 cups dressing

Level: Easy

Ingredients:

* 2 large shallots diced finely

* ! tablespoon Dijon mustard

* 2 tablespoons zinfandel vinegar

* 2 tablespoons sherry vinegar

* 1/2 cups extra virgin olive oil

* 1/2 cup vegetable oil

* sea salt and fresh cracked pepper (to taste)

Directions:

In a small bowl whisk together all ingredients , salt and pepper to taste. Place in covered container and refrigerate until needed.

This can be made days ahead and stored in refrigerator .

Spiced Caramelized Pecans

Prep: 5 minutes

Cook 5 minutes

Yields: 2 cups

Level: Easy

Ingredients:

* 2 cups peanut oil

* 2 cups whole pecans

* 1 teaspoon Kosher salt

* 1/2 teaspoon cayenne pepper

* 1 cup sifted confectioners sugar

Directions:

In a deep pot heat oil to 350 degrees. Use a candy thermometer to check temperature. Slowly add pecans and deep fry for about 1 minute. Transfer to glass or metal bowl and season with mixture of powdered sugar and spices . Coat and shake until all sugar and spice mixture has coated pecans. Transfer to backing sheet and allow to cool . DO NOT USE YOUR HANGS TO TOSSPECANS. A wooden spoon is recommended as pecans will be extremely hot.

These pecans can also be dished up and served as a cocktail snack they are so delicious

Octopus Salad with Spiced Cucumber

Prep: 15 minutes

Inactive: 1 hour in refrigerator

Cook: 35 minutes

Serves: 6 to 8

Level: Intermediate

Ingredients:

* 1 1/2 to 2 pounds fresh or frozen octopus

* 1/2 cup English cucumber

* 1/4 cup Spanish (red) onion sliced thinly

* 3 cloves garlic peeled and minced

* 2 table spoons sambal

* 2 tablespoons sea salt

* 1 teaspoon fresh cracked black pepper

* 1/2 cup extra virgin olive oil

* 2 tablespoons white balsamic vinegar

* 1/4 cup fresh squeezed lemon juice

* 2 vine ripe heirloom tomatoes , diced

* 2 tablespoons minced chives

Directions:

Before cooking remove tentacles and cartilage inside and rinse very well. Over high heat in large pot bring 10 cups water to boil and add octopus. Cook until slightly pink and remove to drain excess water. Cool and chop into small bite sized pieces. Set aside .

In a large bowl add all ingredients except octopus, tomato and chives. Combine well but do not bruise cucumbers. Add in octopus and tomatoes tossing lightly . Once again do not bruise cucumbers or tomatoes. Refrigerate 1 to 2 hours until very well chilled . Transfer to serving dish and add diced chives to garnish and serve.

* For a different variation add cooked and chopped shrimp or butter clams or both*

Warm Duck Salad

Prep: 15 minutes

Cook: 20 minutes

Serves: 4 to 6

Level: Easy

Ingredients:

* 2 boneless duck breasts skin on (about 12 to 14 ounces each)

* Kosher salt

* fresh cracked pepper

* 1 tablespoon minced shallots

* 2 1/2 tablespoons good quality sherry vinegar

* 1 teaspoon orange zest

* 1/2 cups good quality extra virgin olive oil

* 3 heads Belgian endive cleaned well

* 1 to heads baby butter lettuce or other delicate baby lettuce

* 2 (10 to 12 ounce) cans very good quality Mandarin orange segments

* 1/2 pint fresh raspberries cleaned

* 1 cup toasted pecan halves

Directions:

Preheat oven to 400 degrees.

Place duck breasts on sheet pan skin side up. Sprinkle with salt and fresh cracked pepper. Roast about 20 to 25 minutes until medium rare. Remove from oven and cover tightly and let rest for 10 to 15 minutes. Remove and discard drippings and skin. Slice each breast then turn sideways to Julienne into smaller pieces.

Meanwhile in a small bowl, combine shallots, sherry vinegar, orange zest and 1 1/2 teaspoons of salt. Whisk in the olive oil till well incorporated. Set aside.

Core the selected lettuces and cut into bite sized pieces. Place in large salad bowl add the raspberries. orange segments and pecans. Add dressing to taste and gently fold in the warm duck and serve immediately.

- This is a delicious salad to serve with any holiday or special occasion dinner party*

Macaroni Salad

Prep: 15 minutes

Cook: 10 to 12

Serves: 6 to 8

Level: Easy

Ingredients:

* 1 pound elbow macaroni

* 3 hard boiled eggs diced

* 2 celery ribs minced

* 1 cup grated sharp cheddar cheese

* 1 red bell pepper seeded and minced

* 1 red onion minced

* 1 cup sweet pickles chopped

* 1 1/4 cup mayonnaise

* 1 tablespoon pickle juice

* 1 ½ tablespoons Dijon mustard

* Kosher salt

* freshly ground black pepper

Directions:

Cook the pasta in salted water according to the package directions, Drain in a colander and rinse under cold water until cooled. Shake the colander to toss the pasta, and drain for about 5 minutes, tossing occasionally.

Transfer the drained pasta to a large bowl and add the eggs, celery, red bell pepper, red onion, sweet pickles, and cheddar cheese.

In a small bowl Mix the mayonnaise, pickle juice, sugar, and Dijon mustard and season with kosher salt and freshly ground black pepper.

Add to the macaroni mix and toss until evenly coated. Season with more salt and pepper to taste and refrigerate for 1 hour before serving.

This is another of those side dish's I am sure we all have had at least once in our lives. Add your own personal touch simply by adding an additional ingredient. My personal favorite is 1/4 teaspoon celery seed. It is a great touch and adds just that little something a lot of Macaroni Salads are missing.

Classic Potato Salad

Prep: 45

Cook: 15

Serves 6 to 8

Level: Easy

Ingredients:

* 1 1/2 pounds russet potatoes, quartered

* 1/2 cup finely chopped white onion

* 1/4 cup finely chopped celery

* 1/4 cup sweet pickle relish

* 3 hard-cooked large eggs, coarsely chopped

* 1/2 cup real mayonnaise

* 2 tablespoon Dijon mustard

* Sea salt

* Fresh cracked pepper

* 1/2 teaspoon celery seed

Directions:

Cook potatoes in boiling water 25 minutes or until potatoes are tender; drain and cool completely.

Cut potatoes into 1/2-inch cubes. Combine potatoes, onion, celery, relish, and eggs in a large bowl.

Combine mayonnaise and remaining ingredients in a small bowl. Pour over the potato mixture, tossing gently to coat.

Cover and refrigerate at least 8 hours.

Classic dish for any dinner or pot luck. Add chopped sweet pickles and reduce relish by half for a different version on this old favorite. As a child in the mid-west during the summer this salad was always on the table regardless who we were visiting for dinner.

Four Bean Salad

Prep: 20

Serves: 6 to 8

Level: Easy

Ingredients:

* 1 (10 ounce) can black beans drained

* 1 (10 ounce) can dark red kidney beans drained

* 1 (10 ounce) can light red kidney beans drained

* 1 (10 ounce) can white beans drained

* 1 stalk celery chopped

* 3 peeled hard boiled eggs , chopped

* 1 medium onion chopped

* 1 small yellow bell pepper chopped fine

* 1 small sweet red pepper chopped fine

* 1/4 cup finely chopped sweet pickles

* sea salt

* Fresh cracked pepper

* 1 8 ounce bottle of Russian dressing

Directions:

In a medium glass bowl combine all ingredients and toss with dressing, salt and pepper to taste. Refrigerate at least 6 hours until well chilled.

* A very easy but delicious salad any one would love. My Great Auntie served this and I remember her insisting I try at least one bite. Which reluctantly I did and it is now one of my favorite side dish's. Please do not put the usual green bean addition, which is more common, try this recipe first and you will soon be a convert to this variation.*

Beer Cheese Soup

Prep: 10 minutes

Cook: 8 to 10 minutes

Serves: 2

Level: Easy

Ingredients:

* 2 tbsp. unsalted butter

* 3 large shallots, minced

* 1 medium carrot, coarsely shredded

* 1 medium onion, minced

* 1/3 cup flour

* 1 3/4 cups vegetable stock

* 1 cup milk

* 1 tsp. caraway seeds, crushed

* Kosher salt and freshly ground black pepper, to taste

* 10 oz. shredded sharp cheddar cheese

* 6 oz. beer, preferably ale

* Gorgonzola cheese, to taste

Directions:

Melt butter in a 4-qt. saucepan over medium-high; add shallots, carrot, and onion and cook until soft, 4 minutes.

Add flour and cook 2 minutes more; add stock, milk, caraway seeds, salt, and pepper and cook until thick, 8-10 minutes.

Add cheddar and beer and cook until cheese has melted, 2-3 minutes. Add Gorgonzola to taste and serve with bread.

*For an even more impressive soup serve in a sourdough bread bowl and enjoy. Do not worry moms the alcohol burns off so no drunk guests with this recipe. *

ENTREES

Braised Pork In The Black Brasato Di Maiale Nero

Prep: 40 minutes

Cook: 2 hours 25 minutes

Serves 6 to 8

Level: Intermediate

Ingredients:

* 1 (4 pound) pork loin tied at regular intervals with butcher's twin

* 2 teaspoon Kosher salt

* 8 fresh sage leaves

* 2 1/2 ounces pancetta

* 3 cloves of garlic crushed

* 1/4 cup flat parsley leaves

* 1/4 cup extra virgin olive oil

* 2 cups red wine (if you would not drink the wine at dinner do not use to cook with)

* 1 (28 ounce) can crushed tomatoes in juice * fresh cracked black pepper

Directions:

Season the pork loin with salt and pepper. Place the sage leaves around the loin and under the twine . Set aside for 30 minutes.

Mince together the pancetta, garlic and parsley to make a very smooth mixture. You can use a food processor for this step. In a large Dutch oven heat the oil and add Pancetta garlic mixture and cook until melted into the oil. Add pork loin and brown until all sides are covered in mixture evenly crusted. Remove loin and set aside. Add 1 cup of the red wine and reduce by half. Add remaining wine and the tomatoes and pork loin, Reduce heat and simmer 2 hours until meat is fork tender.

remove from Dutch oven and allow to rest 15 minutes then remove twine and sage leaves. Cut into 1 inch slices and serve.

Oven roasted vegetables of your choice pare well with this along side a rice pilaf or baked potato. Forget the diet on this one and just enjoy as a special meal or cold as a great variation on the every day sandwich

Beef Short Ribs

Ingredients:

* 6 beef short ribs trimmed of fat

* Kosher salt

* Fresh ground black pepper

* 1/4 extra virgin olive oil

* 1 small fennel bulb ,fronds, core and stems removed. large diced

* 1 leek well cleaned and white part only large diced

* 1 1/2 cups white onion diced

* 4 cups celery large diced

* 2 carrots large diced

* 3 garlic cloves minced

* 2 tablespoons tomato paste

* 1 (750 ml) good quality extra dry red wine

* Fresh rosemary sprigs

* Fresh thyme sprigs

* 1 tablespoon light brown sugar

* 6 cups beef stock

Directions:

Preheat oven to 400 degrees and place ribs on sheet pan and roast for 15 to 20 minutes. Remove from the oven and reduce temperature to 300 degrees.

Meanwhile place the olive oil in large cast iron Dutch oven add fennel, leeks, onion, celery and carrots and cook over medium low heat for about 20 minutes. Add the garlic and cook another 2 minutes. Add the tomato paste and red wine and bring to a boil and reduce by half about 10 minutes. Add1 teaspoon each salt and pepper. Tie the rosemary and thyme together with butchers twin and add to pot. Add the roasted ribs and beef stock to pot and reduce heat to low and simmer 2 hours until the meat is very tender.

Remove the ribs carefully along with rosemary and thyme sprigs . return pot to heat and reduce remaining ingredients by half. Return ribs to pot and heat through. Serve immediately.

Very rich and hearty dish . Serve with your favorite side dish's and fresh green salad for a comforting winter meal

Roast Turkey with Oyster Dressing

Prep: 40 minutes

Cook: 3 to 5 hours

Yields: 6 to 10 servings

Level: Easy

Ingredients:

* 10 to 12 pound Turkey

* sea salt

* Fresh ground pepper

* 1/4 cup olive oil

* 1 1/2 cups chopped onions

* 1 cup chopped celery

* 1 pound stale corn bread crumbled

* 8 ounce oyster crackers crumbled

* 1 1/2 teaspoons thyme (dried)

* 1 teaspoon dried sage

* 2 eggs lightly beaten

* 1 pint of small oysters with liquid

Directions:

Clean the turkey well removing giblets and any excess fat inside. Salt and pepper inside and out. Set aside in large roasting pan.

Meanwhile in a large bowl combine all ingredients mixing well. Salt and pepper to taste. From large opening in turkey fill cavity with the cornbread mixture packing cavity well. With heavy thread sew flap over opening to cover cavity. Completely cover turkey with real unsalted butter and cover with moistened flour sack type towel. Allow towel to drape turkey and enough to lay in bottom of pan. Cover with heavy tin foil to keep towel from burning Baste the bird with butter and pan drippings about every 30 minutes. Re-wet towel as needed. When turkey is cooked through remove foil and towel and allow skin to brown before serving.

*Using an old flour sack towel (moistened) while baking helps wick up juices from the bottom of pan and keeps turkey moist and delicious. This is a method used for 100 plus years on the prairies , country homes and farms of the

US. Try it you will be amazed how moist your turkey will turn out when done right.*

New Orleans Braised Pork Belly

Prep: 2 hours

Inactive: 24 hours/24 hours

Cook: 2 hours and 30 minutes

Serves: 6 to 8

Level: Intermediate

Ingredients:

* 2 (2 1/2 lb) slabs pork belly

* 2 cups fresh squeezed orange juice (canned or bottled will not do)

* 1 cup soy sauce

* 1 packed cup light brown sugar

* 1/2 cup fresh squeezed lemon juice

* 1/3 cup minced garlic

* 1/4 minced ginger

* 1/4 cup minced green onions (white parts only)

* 4 cups chicken stock

* 12 ounces frisse lettuce cleaned and spun dry

* 1/2 cup rice wine vinegar

* Sea salt

* Fresh cracked pepper

Directions:

Place each section of pork belly in 1 1/2 gallon plastic resealable bag. Combine all ingredients except chicken stock and pour half of mixture into each bag . Refrigerate over night. In the morning remove and allow to come to room temperature . About 2 to 3 hours.

Preheat oven to 325 egress'

Remove pork belly from bags and place skin side up into roasting pan. Add chicken stock and marinade to almost cover bellies. Roast for 1 hour then turn over and roast 1 1/2 hours more. Remove from oven and allow to cool. After cool remove skin and any congealed fat. Refrigerate over night wrapped tightly in plastic wrap.

Preheat oven to 400 degrees.

Remove pork belly from the refrigerator and again remove any congealed fats . Place in glass baking dish and cook in oven until warmed through.

Not a dish for the super health conscience, but a delicious taste of New Orleans for the rest of us

Chicken Piccata with Lemon, Capers and Artichoke Hearts

Prep: 15 minutes

Cook: 10 minutes

Serves: 4

Level: Easy

Ingredients:

* 4 (4ounce) boneless skinless chicken breast halves

* Kosher salt

* Fresh cracked pepper

* 1/3 cup all purpose flour

* 1/2 teaspoon lemon zest

* 1/2 teaspoon paprika

* 1/2 teaspoon garlic powder

* 1 tablespoon olive oil

* 1/4 cup fresh squeezed lemon juice

* 1/2 cup dry white wine

* 1/2 cup reduced sodium chicken broth

* 1 (14 ounce) can artichoke hearts

* 1/4 cup drained caper * 1 cup cooked brown rice

* 1/2 cup frozen lima beans thawed

Directions:

Place chicken breasts in zip lock bags and pound with meat mallet or rolling pin until 1/4 inch thick. Remove from bag and season all over. In a plastic bag or shallow pan combine flour, lemon zest, paprika and garlic powder. Mix well. Add chicken and coat each breast well. Remove and shack of excess flour.

Heat oil in large skillet over medium high heat. Add chicken and brown 2 minutes on each side. Cook until coked through and golden brown. Add lemon juice, white wine, and chicken broth and bring to a simmer. Simmer 5 minutes until sauce thickens. Add artichoke hearts and capers and simmer 2 minutes until heated through.

Cook rice according to package directions adding Lima beans at beginning of cooking process. Serve chicken with sauce over rice.

Even if you dislike artichoke hearts try this one , it will change your mind.

Pasta Puttanesca

Prep: 30 minutes

Cook: 1 hour

Serves: 4 to 6

Level: Intermediate

Ingredients:

* 2 teaspoons chopped and smashed anchovies

* 2 teaspoons capers rinsed and chopped finely

* 1 1/2 cups seasoned tomato sauce

* 1/4 cups unsalted clam juice

* Freshly cracked pepper

* 1 1/2 tablespoons hot chili paste (recommend Peperoncino Piccante Chile "Paste")

* 1 1/2 cups seeded and peeled fresh tomatoes

* 1/2 half cup each Kalamata and Picoline olives pitted and quartered

* 1/2 teaspoons dried oregano

* 2 tablespoons chopped Italian parsley

* 1 1/2 teaspoons dry red wine

* 2 tablespoons extra virgin olive oil

* 2 pounds fresh pasta of your choice (I recommend bow tie, rigatoni, or thin spaghetti)

* 1/4 fresh grated Pecorino cheese

Directions:

With the flat side of a knife smash anchovies until smooth. After capers are rinsed and dried do the same with them.

In a medium sauce pan combine all ingredients except pasta and cheese and bring to a boil. Reduce heat and simmer for about 1 hour to blend flavors completely.

In a large heavy pot boil enough water to cook pasta till cooked but slightly firm state.

Drain and toss with sauce to coat evenly.

Grate Pecorino cheese over pasta and Serve immediately..

As my 2 idols Albert Einstein and Martha Stewart have said "Simple, But not to simple"

New York Deli Style Corned Beef

Prep: 20 minutes

Inactive: 10 days

Cook: 3 hours

Serves 6 to 8

Level: Easy

Ingredients:

* 2 quarts water

* 1 cup Kosher salt

* 1/2 cup brown sugar

* 2 tablespoons saltpeter

* 1 cinnamon stick broke into pieces

* 1 teaspoon mustard seed

* 1 teaspoon black pepper corns

* 8 whole cloves

* 8 whole allspice berries

* 12 juniper berries

* 2 bay leaves crumbled

* 1/2 teaspoon dried ginger

* 2 pounds ice

* 1 (4 to 5 pound) brisket, trimmed.

* 1 small onion quartered

* 1 large carrot cut up

* 1 stalk celery cut up

Directions:

In a large pot combine all ingredients and boil for 10 minutes until all flavors are combined. Remove from heat and add ice to cool. Put brisket in large refrigerator container and cover with liquid. Refrigerate 10 days , checking daily to assure brisket is submerged completely.

After 10 days remove from refrigerator and rinse well under cold water . Place the brisket in a pot with carrots, celery and onion and add enough water to cover by 1 inch. Set over high heat and bring to a rolling boil. Reduce heat to low and simmer 2 to 2 1/2 hours until meat is for tender.

*Remove from pot and slice across the grain and serve with boiled cabbage and potatoes or chill and serve as sandwiches on rye bread or warm on grilled pumpernickel bread with

warm sauerkraut and melted Swiss cheese as a classic
Reuben.*

Fettuccine Alfredo

Prep: 15 minutes

Cook: 40 minutes

Serves: 4

Level: Intermediate

Ingredients:

* 2 pounds fettuccine pasta

* 1 pint heavy cream

* 1/2 cup (1stick) unsalted sweet cream butter

* 1 cup freshly grated Parmigiano Reggiano cheese

* Freshly cracked black pepper

* Chopped flat-leafed parsley , for garnish

Directions:

Heat heavy cream over low heat in deep sauté pan. Add butter and whisk gently to melt. Sprinkle in cheese and whisk to incorporate completely. Season with fresh cracked pepper. Remove from heat.

In large pot bring plenty of boiling water to a rolling boil. Add pasta and a pinch of sea salt. Cook pasta until tender but firm to bite. Remove from heat and drain immediately. Transfer to sauce pan and toss gently to cover completely with warm sauce.

Transfer to warm serving platter and top with grated cheeses and parsley. Serve immediately.

This can be served with grilled chicken or your choice of shell fish. Or for a more upscale elegant dish , for those very special occasions add lobster meat or your choice of crab meat.

Southern Fried Chicken

Prep: 15 minutes

Cook: 20 minutes

Serves: 4

Level: Easy

Ingredients:

* 1 teaspoon pepper

* 1 tablespoon dried thyme

* 1 tablespoon paprika

* 2 teaspoons salt

* 2 teaspoons garlic powder

* 1 large egg

* 1/3 cup whole milk

* 2 tablespoons fresh lemon juice

* 1 broiler/fryer chicken (3 to 4 pounds), cut up

* Oil for deep-fat frying

* 1-3/4 cups all-purpose flour

* 2/3 cup corn meal

Directions:

In a shallow bowl, mix the first five ingredients. In a separate shallow bowl, whisk egg, milk and lemon juice until blended. Dip chicken in flour/cornmeal mixture to coat all sides; shake off excess. Dip in egg mixture, then again in flour mixture/cornmeal .

In an large cast iron (cast iron is the preferred method) skillet or deep fryer, heat oil to 375°. Fry chicken, a few pieces at a time, 6-8 minutes on each side or until golden brown and chicken juices run clear. Drain on paper towels. And serve piping hot.

*This delicious chicken is great for Sunday dinner served piping hot with mashed potatoes and pan dripping gravy or chilled for a delightful lunch or picnic item.

The key to a crispy non soggy chicken is the addition of the cornmeal and a good scald, so assure oil is to temperature.*

Yankee Pot Roast

Prep: 30 min.

Cook: 7 hours

Serves: 8

Level: Easy

Ingredients:

* 1 can (14-1/2 ounces) beef broth

* 3 medium potatoes (about 1 pound), cut into 1-1/2-inch cubes

* 2 medium turnips (about 9 ounces), cut into 1-1/2-inch pieces

* 4 medium carrots, cut into 1/2-inch pieces

* 1 large onion, cut into 1-inch wedges

* 2 celery ribs, cut into 1/2-inch pieces

* 1 tablespoon olive oil

* 1 boneless beef chuck roast (about 3 pounds)

* 1 teaspoon sea salt

* 1/2 teaspoon fresh cracked pepper

* 3 tablespoons cornstarch

* 3 tablespoons cold water

Directions:

In a small saucepan, bring broth to a boil; remove from heat. Add tea bags; steep, covered, 3-5 minutes according to taste. Discard tea bags. Meanwhile, combine vegetables in a 6-qt. slow cooker.

In a large skillet, heat oil over medium-high heat; brown roast on all sides. Place over vegetables; pour broth over top. Sprinkle roast with salt and pepper; Cook, covered, on low until beef and vegetables are tender, 7-9 hours.

Remove roast and vegetables from slow cooker; keep warm.

Transfer cooking juices to a saucepan; skim fat. Bring juices to a boil. In a small bowl, mix cornstarch and water until smooth; stir into juices. Return to a boil, stirring constantly; cook and stir until thickened, 1-2 minutes. Serve with roast and vegetables.

* A classic comfort food we all remember from at least one special occasion in our childhood years*

Meat Loaf & Yukon Gold Mashed Potatoes

Prep: 30 minutes

Cook: 4 Hours

Serves: 8 to 10

Level: Easy

Ingredients:

* 1-1/2 cups beef stock, divided

* 3 slices white bread, torn into small pieces

* 2 large button mushrooms (about 6 ounces), cut into chunks

* 1 medium onion, cut into wedges

* 3 garlic cloves, halved

* 2 large eggs, lightly beaten

* 1-1/2 pounds ground beef

* !/2 pound ground pork

* 2 tablespoons Worcestershire sauce

* Sea salt

* Fresh cracked pepper

* 1/2 cup ketchup

* 2 tablespoons tomato paste

* 2 tablespoons brown sugar

* 6 medium Yukon gold potatoes

* 1/2 stick real butter

* 1/4 half and half (for mashed potatoes)

Directions:

Finely chop mushrooms, onion, carrot, celery and garlic. In large mixing bowl add vegetable mixture, eggs, beef, pork, Worcestershire sauce, 1-1/4 teaspoons salt and 3/4 teaspoon pepper to bread mixture; mix lightly but thoroughly. Place meat mixture in a 10 x 13 glass baking dish forming meat mixture into a loaf leaving about 2 inch's on all sides..

Mix together glaze ingredients ketchup, tomato paste and brown; spread over loaf.

Cook, uncovered, on low until a thermometer reads 160°, 1 1/2 to 2 hours. Using a turkey baster, remove and discard liquid contained in foil; lifting with foil, remove meat loaf to a platter Let stand 10 minutes before cutting.

Meanwhile in a medium sauce pan boil peeled potatoes until fork tender. Drain water; transfer potatoes to large bowl. Mash with potato masher (I prefer not using mixer unless you prefer super whipped not mashed potatoes), gradually adding butter, salt and pepper and half and half.

Chill unused meatloaf for delicious meatloaf sandwiches any one would enjoy. Left over mashed potatoes can also be used for potato pancakes.

Stuffed Cabbage Rolls

Prep: 20 minutes

Cook: 6 hours

Serves: 6

Level: Easy

Ingredients

* 12 cabbage leaves

* 1 cup cooked brown rice

* 1/4 cup finely chopped onion

* 1 large egg, lightly beaten

* 1/4 cup fat-free milk

* 1/2 teaspoon salt

* 1 pound lean ground beef (90% lean)

* 1 can (8 ounces) tomato sauce

* 1 tablespoon brown sugar

* 1 tablespoon lemon juice

* 1 teaspoon Worcestershire sauce□ 1/4 teaspoon pepper

Directions:

In batches, cook cabbage in boiling water 3-5 minutes or until crisp-tender. Drain; cool slightly. Trim the thick vein from the bottom of each cabbage leaf, making a V-shaped cut.

In a large bowl, combine rice, onion, egg, milk, salt and pepper. Add beef; mix lightly but thoroughly. Place about 1/4 cup beef mixture on each cabbage leaf. Pull together cut edges of leaf to overlap; fold over filling. Fold in sides and roll up.

Place six rolls in a 4- or 5-qt. slow cooker, seam side down.

In a bowl, mix tomato sauce, lemon juice, brown sugar and Worcestershire sauce and pour half of the sauce over cabbage rolls. Top with remaining rolls and sauce.

Cook, covered, on low 6-8 hours or until a thermometer inserted in beef reads 160° and cabbage is tender.

Not a quick dinner but well worth the wait even for those that usually do not like cabbage

Chicken Cordon Bleu

Prep: 20 minutes

Bake: 30 minutes

Serves: 8

Level: Easy

Ingredients:

* 8 boneless skinless chicken breast halves (4 ounces each)

* 1/4 teaspoon sea salt

* 1/8 teaspoon fresh cracked pepper

* 3 tablespoons butter
* 1 package (17.3 ounces) frozen puff pastry, thawed

* 8 slices Swiss cheese

* 8 slices fully cooked ham

* 1 large egg

* 1 tablespoon water

Directions:

Sprinkle chicken with salt and pepper. In a large skillet, brown chicken in butter for 1-2 minutes on each side. Remove to paper towels to drain.

On a lightly floured surface, roll each pastry sheet into a 12-in. square. Cut into four 6-in. squares. Place a chicken breast in the center of each square; top with cheese and ham.

Whisk egg and water; lightly brush over pastry edges. Bring two sides of pastry over chicken, overlapping one over the other; press seams to seal. Pinch together ends and fold under.

Transfer to a greased 15x10x1-in. baking pan; brush tops with egg mixture.

Bake at 400° for 30 minutes or until a thermometer reads 165°.

This is a delightful dish to serve on a luncheon buffet. Chilled and served on fresh French bread, lettuce and tomato makes a unexpected surprise for a midday sandwich.

Stuffed Clams

Prep: 1 hour

Bake: 20 minutes

Serves: 6 to 10

Level: Easy

Ingredients:

* 20 fresh large quahog clams (about 10 pounds)

* 1 pound Fully Cooked Andouille Sausage

* 1 large onion, chopped (about 2 cups)

* 3 teaspoons seafood seasoning (Old Bay suggested)

* 1 package (14 ounces) herb stuffing cubes

* 1 cup water

* Lemon wedges, optional

* Hot pepper sauce, optional

Directions:

Add 2 in. of water to a stockpot. Add clams and Old Bay seasoning; bring to a boil. Cover and steam 15-20 minutes or until clams open.

Remove clams and sausage from pot, reserving 2 cups cooking liquid; cool slightly. Discard any unopened clams.

Preheat oven broiler

Remove clam meat from shells. Separate shells; reserve 30 half shells for stuffing. Place clam meat in a food processor; process until finely chopped. Transfer to a large bowl.

Remove casings from sausage; cut sausage into 1-1/2-in. pieces. Place in a food processor; process until finely chopped. Add sausage, onion and seafood seasoning to chopped clams. Stir in stuffing cubes. Add reserved cooking liquid and enough water to reach desired moistness, about 1 cup.

Spoon clam mixture into reserved shells. Place in 15x10x1-in. baking pans. Bake 15-20 minutes or until heated through. Preheat broiler.

Broil clams 4-5 minutes or until golden brown. Serve with lemon wedges and hot pepper sauce..

Frito Pie

Prep: 10 minutes

Cook: 20 minutes

Serves: 6

Level: Easy

Ingredients:

* 1 pound ground beef

* 1 medium onion, chopped

* 2 cans (15 ounces each) Ranch Style beans (pinto beans in seasoned tomato sauce)

* 1 package (9-3/4 ounces) Fritos corn chips

* 2 cans (10 ounces each) enchilada sauce

* 2 cups shredded cheddar cheese

* Thinly sliced green onions, optional

Direction:

Preheat oven to 350°.

In a large skillet, cook beef and onion over medium heat 6-8 minutes or until beef is no longer pink and onion is tender, breaking up beef into crumbles; drain. Stir in beans; heat through.

Reserve 1 cup corn chips for topping. Place remaining corn chips in a greased 13x9-in. baking dish. Layer with meat mixture, enchilada sauce and cheese; top with reserved chips.

Bake, uncovered, 15-20 minutes or until cheese is melted. If desired, sprinkle with green onions

This recipe was given to me by our lunch lady at Spartanburg High School (rural Indiana) in the 1960's. She said that her lunch lady had also passed it on some 30 plus years earlier.

Pecan-Crusted Chicken Nuggets

Prep: 15 minutes

Cook: 15 minutes

Serves: 6

Level: Easy

Ingredients:

* 1-1/2 cups cornflakes

* 1 tablespoon dried parsley flakes

* 1 teaspoon salt

* 1/2 teaspoon garlic powder

* 1/2 cup panko (Japanese) bread crumbs

* 1/2 cup finely chopped pecans

* 3 tablespoons 2% milk

* 1-1/2 pounds boneless skinless chicken breasts, cut into 1-inch pieces

* Cooking spray

* 1/2 teaspoon pepper

Directions:

Preheat oven to 400°.

Place cornflakes, parsley, salt, garlic powder and pepper in a blender; cover and pulse until finely ground. Transfer to a shallow bowl; stir in bread crumbs and pecans. Place milk in another shallow bowl. Dip chicken in milk, then roll in crumb mixture to coat.

Place on a greased baking sheet; spritz chicken with cooking spray. Bake 12-15 minutes or until chicken is no longer pink, turning once halfway through cooking.

Great new take on every Child's favorite chicken nuggets.

Oysters Bienville

Prep: 15 minutes

Cook: 15 to 20 minutes

Serves: 4 to 6 (or 12 as a starter)

Level: Intermediate

Ingredients:

* Rock salt

* 12 fresh oysters on the half shell

* ⅓ cup panko (Japanese bread crumbs)

* 2 tablespoons freshly grated Parmesan cheese

* 3 tablespoons olive oil

* ¼ cup minced white onion

* 1 clove garlic, minced

* ¼ cup finely chopped white mushrooms

* ¼ cup finely chopped fresh shrimp

* 2 tablespoons white wine

* ½ teaspoon salt

* ¼ teaspoon ground black pepper

* 1 tablespoon all-purpose flour

* 3 tablespoons chicken broth

* 3 tablespoons 2% reduced-fat milk

* 1 large egg yolk, lightly beaten

* Garnish: sliced green onion, lemon wedges

Directions:

Preheat oven to 400°.

In an 13x9-inch baking dish, spread a ¾-inch layer of rock salt. Arrange oysters on top of rock salt.

In a medium bowl, combine bread crumbs and Parmesan. Set aside.

In a large saucepan, heat oil over medium-high heat. Add onion; cook until tender, about 2 minutes.

Add garlic, mushrooms, shrimp, wine, salt, and pepper. Cook until mushrooms are tender and shrimp are pink and firm, 2 to 3 minutes.

Sprinkle with flour; cook for 1 minute, stirring constantly. Add broth, and stir to combine. Add milk; cook until creamy and slightly thickened. Remove from heat, and slowly add egg yolk, stirring constantly.

Spoon about 1 tablespoon shrimp mixture onto each oyster, and top with bread crumb mixture.

Bake until tops are lightly browned, 16 to 18 minutes.

Garnish with green onion and lemon, if desired. Serve immediately.

* This New Orleans classic is sure to be a hit with your friends, family and guests at any special occasion. One of my personal favorites I will always remember my Mother making this dish every time I requested them. I now follow tradition with my friends and family making them as often as I am requested and sometimes now that the kids are all grown and gone I will make a batch for just me. I am worth the effort , besides each time I make them it brings back so many wonderful memories of my Mother.*

Tuna Noodle Casserole

Prep: 10 minutes

Cook: 30 minutes

Serves: 4 to 5

Level: Easy

Ingredients:

* 1 can (10-3/4 ounces) condensed cream of mushroom soup, undiluted

* 3/4 cup milk

* 2 cups cooked (wide) egg noodles

* 1 cup frozen peas, thawed

* 2 cans (8 ounces) solid albacore packed tuna, drained and flaked

* 2 tablespoons dry bread crumbs

* 2 tablespoon unsalted butter, melted

Directions:

Preheat oven to 400 degrees

In a large bowl, combine soup and milk until smooth. Add the noodles, peas, and tuna; mix well.

Pour into a 1-1/2-qt. baking dish coated with cooking spray. Bake, uncovered, for 25 minutes.

Toss bread crumbs and butter; sprinkle over the top. Bake 5 minutes longer or until golden brown.

This is one of those mid-west dish's I am sure most of us remember. Try topping the casserole with grated cheddar cheese for a different spin on an old favorite.

South-West Polenta Casserole

Prep: 2 1/2 hours

Cook: 55 to 60 minutes

Serves: 6

Level: Easy

Ingredients:

* 1 cup yellow cornmeal

* 1 teaspoon salt

* 4 cups water, divided

* 1 pound ground beef

* 1 cup chopped onion

* 1/2 cup chopped green pepper

* 2 garlic cloves, minced

* 1 can (14-1/2 ounces) diced tomatoes, with juice

* 1 can (8 ounces) tomato sauce

* 1/2 pound sliced fresh mushrooms

* 1 teaspoon each dried basil

* 1 teaspoon minced fresh basil

* Dash hot pepper sauce

* 2 cups shredded mozzarella cheese

* 1/4 cup grated Parmesan cheese

Directions:

For polenta, in a small bowl, whisk cornmeal, salt and 1 cup water until smooth. In a large saucepan, bring remaining water to a boil. Add cornmeal mixture, stirring constantly. Bring to a boil; cook and stir for 3 minutes or until thickened.

Reduce heat to low; cover and cook for 15 minutes. Divide mixture between two greased 8-in. square baking dishes. Cover and refrigerate until firm, about 1-1/2 hours.

In a large cast iron skillet, cook the beef, onion, green pepper and garlic over medium heat until meat is no longer pink; drain. Stir in the tomatoes, tomato sauce, mushrooms, herbs and hot pepper sauce; bring to a boil. Reduce heat; simmer, uncovered, for 20 minutes or until thickened.

Loosen one polenta from sides and bottom of dish; invert onto a waxed paper-lined baking sheet and set aside. Spoon half of the meat mixture over the remaining polenta. Sprinkle with half the mozzarella and half the Parmesan cheese. Top with reserved polenta and remaining meat mixture.

Preheat oven to 350 degrees.

Cover and bake for 40 minutes or until heated through.
Uncover; sprinkle with remaining cheese.

Bake 10 minutes longer or until cheese is melted.

Let stand for 10 minutes before cutting.

* This dish I first remember having in Flagstaff Arizona
when I was 15 at the home of some very special Mexican-
American friends from school, on of all days Thanksgiving.
It has been a tradition in my home since the first year I did
Thanksgiving on my own . Always a delight to hear the
reactions of friends and family.*

Charcoal Grilled Herb Rabbit

Prep: 1 hour 30 minutes

Cook: 30 minutes

Serves: 4

Level: Easy

Ingredients:

* 1 (3- to 4-pound) rabbit, cut into 8 pieces

* 8 sprigs fresh thyme, leaves picked

* 4 sprigs fresh rosemary, leaves picked

* 4 cloves garlic, peeled

* ½ cup extra-virgin olive oil

* 1 lemon, zested and juiced

* 1 teaspoon honey

* ½ teaspoon kosher salt

* ½ teaspoon Fresh cracked black pepper

Directions:

In a large bowl or gallon-size resealable bag, place rabbit pieces

.

In the container of a blender, combine thyme, rosemary, garlic, oil, lemon zest and juice, and honey; process until smooth. Pour marinade over rabbit; cover and refrigerate for at least 1 hour.

Preheat grill to medium-high heat (350° to 400°).

Remove rabbit from marinade, and sprinkle with salt and pepper. Reserve marinade. Grill rabbit legs for 10 minutes, turning occasionally. Add loin and ribs; grill 20 minutes more, continuing to turn all pieces occasionally and brushing with reserved marinade.

Garnish with rosemary and thyme, if desired.

This is also a great way to grill chicken or even pork chops..

Mom's Chicken Plus

Prep : 15 minutes

Cook : 15 minutes

Serves: 4

Level: Intermediate

INGREDIENTS:

* 1½ pounds boneless skinless chicken breast and thigh mix, cut into strips

* ½ teaspoon kosher salt

* ¼ teaspoon freshly ground black pepper

* ¼ teaspoon garlic powder

* ¼ teaspoon dry thyme

* 3 tablespoons extra virgin olive oil, divided

* 4 ounces Walla Walla sweet onion cut into strips

* 4 ounces red or yellow sweet bell pepper cut into strips

* 1 head Kale, stripped from ribs and roughly chopped and rinsed

* ¼ cup good quality Balsamic vinegar

* 1 can pitted black olives, drained and sliced

* 10 sun dried tomatoes (packed in oil variety), cut into strips

* ½ cup chicken stock

* 1 tablespoon cold clarified butter

Directions:

Lay out chicken strips and season both sides with salt, pepper, garlic powder and thyme.

In a very large skillet, over high heat, pour in two tablespoons of the olive oil and let get smoking hot. Piece by piece, lay in half the chicken and cook for about two minutes per side, then remove to a platter. Repeat for remainder of the chicken.

Add the remaining tablespoon of oil and reduce to medium high. Add onions and stir two minutes then add peppers and stir and cook for two additional minutes. Add kale including any water stuck to leaves from rinsing and toss and cook 2 more minutes.

Add vinegar and cook for about two minutes to deglaze. Add olives, tomatoes, stock and cooked chicken, including any liquid from chicken. Cook to reduce liquid, about two minutes, then remove from heat and add cold clarified butter and toss to combine.

Serve immediately.

This is a great way to serve chicken over rice or with buttered noodles. Your family will love it

Great-Grandmothers Chicken & Dumplings

Prep : 1 hour and 15 minutes

Cook: 15 to 20 minutes

Serves: 4 to 6

Level: Easy

Ingredients:

* 1 (4 to 5 pound) whole chicken, thawed, cleaned and giblets removed from inside cavity
* enough water to cover the whole chicken
* 4 celery pieces (celery leaves) included

* 4 carrots cut up

* one onion cut into quarters
* 3 bay leaves
* 1 teaspoon poultry seasoning to taste
* 4 tablespoon unsalted butter (2 for broth and 2 for dumplings)
* garlic powder, to taste
* sea salt and fresh cracked pepper, to taste
* 5 - 6 cups reserved chicken broth or use Swanson's canned chicken broth
* 1 (10 ounce) can cream of chicken soup

* 2 cups all purpose flour (plus extra for dusting)
* 1/2 teaspoon baking powder
* 1 cup water

Directions:

Clean out the inside of the chicken, removing the heart, liver and giblets. Add the whole chicken into a large stock or soup pot.

Add the celery ribs and leaves, carrots, onion, bay leaves, poultry seasoning, butter, garlic powder, salt and pepper. Add enough water to cover the chicken.

Over high heat bring the chicken to a boil, reduce heat, cover (leave a 1 to 2 inch opening for the steam to escape) and simmer on low for 1 hour or until the chicken is cooked through.

Remove the chicken to a cutting board to cool. Strain the broth into a mesh strainer and discard the vegetables and any small bones.

Add 5 cups broth back to the pot, cream of chicken soup and butter. Using a wire whisk mix until the soup is blended.

When the chicken is cool enough, pull all the meat off the bone and add chicken back to the pot with the broth. Discard the chicken bones and prepare the dumplings.

To prepare dumplings: In a medium size bowl, combine the flour, baking powder and salt. Mix to combine. Cut the butter into the flour mixture with a pastry cutter.

Stir in the water or broth and blend until the dough forms

into a soft ball. On a floured surface using a rolling pin, roll out the dumpling dough to 1/4 inch thickness.

Using a pizza cutter, cut the dumplings into 2-3 inch squares. Add the dumplings to a bowl of flour and lightly toss.

Bring the broth to a boil and add the dumplings (shaking off the additional flour before adding). Reduce heat to low. Continue until all the dumplings are coated and added to the broth.

Simmer the dumplings for about 20 minutes, pushing them down with a wooden spoon into the broth every 5 minutes until they no longer float.

Continue cooking until the dumplings are done and the mixture thickens to the desired consistency.

Cool slightly and ladle into bowls.

I believe every Mother and Grand-Mother in the mid-west had a variation of this recipe. I even remember a family friend in Indiana that had butchered her own chickens the day prior to our visit and included the unhatched eggs of said chickens. She had added them to the pot for an incredible surprise.

True Mince Meat Pie

Prep: 1 hour

Cook: 45 minutes to 1 hour

Serves: 8 to 12

Level: Intermediate

Ingredients:

* 1 1/2 pounds leftover beef roast
* 1 1/2 pounds apples
* 1 cup raisins or currants
* 1/2 cup white sugar
* 1/2 cup brown sugar
* 1/8 teaspoon pepper
* 1/2 teaspoon salt
* 2 teaspoons cinnamon
* 1 teaspoon ground clove
* 2 teaspoons fresh ground nutmeg
* 1/4 cup brandy
* 2 cups cider or apple juice
* Double recipe for Pie Crust (use Levi's perfect pie crust recipe)
* 2 tablespoon real sweat cream butter

Directions:

Chop beef very fine, into about ¼-inch pieces.

Pare, core, and chop apples to make 3 cups.

Mix beef, suet, apples, raisins or currants, white and brown sugars, spices, brandy, and cider or apple juice.

Preheat oven to 400 degrees

Prepare pie crust.

Line 2 (9 inch) pie plates with pastry, fill each with half of meat mixture. Cover with top crusts, seal edges, slit holes on top for steam to escape. If desired, spread a thick layer of butter on pastry for flakiest upper crust.

Bake 45 minutes to 1 hour.

Let cool for 15 to 20 minutes before serving.

The first time I remember having this amazing pie I was about 7 years old. I spent the whole day thinking how wonderful the world was that my Granny was cooking a pie as my dinner. Much to my surprise when dinner finally was served, I discovered to my disbelief I had not been told the complete truth and it was not a fruit pie as I dreamed of, but meat. I will never forget the smile on her face after my first bite I asked " I hope I can have seconds Grams?" Some years later she told me almost the same story of a Sunday on the family farm in Michigan and her first "minced pie"

SIDE DISH'S

Mac and cheese

Prep: 10 minutes

Cook: 20 minutes

Serves: 4 to 6

Level: Easy

Ingredients:

* 8 ounces dry pasta (I use bow tie or elbow macaroni)
* 1 small onion
* 2 whole cloves
* 1 tsp salt
* 5 tablespoons butter
* 1/3 cup of freshly grated Parmesan Cheese

* 1 cup grated sharp Wisconsin cheddar

* 1/2 cup crumbled Maytag Blue cheese
* 1/4 teaspoon fresh nutmeg
* 1/3 cup heavy cream
* 1/4 cup of breadcrumbs (optional)

Directions:

Boil noodles with one tablespoon of butter and with the onion studded with two cloves for about 10 minutes (onion and cloves are to be discarded in this recipe, but you can also choose to slice the onion and layer it among the pasta before baking).

Drain and toss the noodles with three more tablespoons of butter, cheeses, nutmeg and cream.

Preheat oven to 350 degrees

Place dressed noodles in a baking dish and cover with bread crumbs and another tablespoon of butter and bake at 350 for 30 minutes.

This recipe comes from a hand written recipe I ran across in some recipes tucked away in my Grandmothers collection it was dated 1834. I have made this numerous times and always get high reviews from family and friends. Makes a great pot luck offering.

Hoppin' John

Prep time: 10 minutes

Cook time: 50 minutes

Serves 4 to 6

Level: Easy

INGREDIENTS:

* 1/3 pound bacon, or 1 ham hock plus 2 Tbsp oil

* 1 celery stalk, diced

* 1 small yellow onion, diced

* 1 small green pepper, diced

* 2 garlic cloves, minced

* 1/2 pound dried black-eyed peas, about 2 cups

* 1 bay leaf

* 2 teaspoons dried thyme

* 1 heaping teaspoon Cajun seasoning

* Salt

* 2 cups long-grain rice

* Scallions or green onions for garnish

Directions:

If you are using bacon, cut it into small pieces and cook it slowly in a medium pot over medium-low heat. If you are using a ham hock, heat the oil in the pot. Once the bacon is crispy (or the oil is hot if you are using a ham hock and not bacon), increase the heat to medium-high and add the celery, onion, and green pepper and sauté until they begin to brown, about 4-5 minutes. Add the garlic, stir well and cook for another 1-2 minutes.

Add the black-eyed peas, bay leaf, thyme and Cajun seasoning and cover with 4 cups of water. If you are using the ham hock, add it to the pot and bring to a simmer. Cook for 30 minutes to an hour, or longer if needed, until the peas are tender.

While the black-eyed peas are cooking, cook the rice separately according to package instructions.

When the peas are tender, strain out the remaining cooking water.

Remove and discard the bay leaf. Taste the peas for salt and add more if needed. If using a ham hock, remove it from the pot, pull off the meat, and return the meat to the pot.

Serve the dish either by placing a ladle-full of black-eyed peas over steamed rice, or by mixing the two together in a large bowl. Garnish with chopped green onions.

A classic side dish which I always serve on New Years day for luck. I was told the luck story of black eyed peas by a grand old southern lady I called Auntie. This ones in her memory.

Louisiana Collard Greens

Prep time: 10 minutes

Cook time: 2 hours

Yield: Serves 4-6

Level: Easy

INGREDIENTS:

* 2 Tbsp bacon fat

* 1 medium onion, sliced

* 1 ham hock

* 2 garlic cloves, minced

* 1 quart chicken broth

* 2 cups water

* 2 pounds chopped collard greens (white parts of stem removed)

* Vinegar and/or Louisiana hot sauce to taste

Directions:

Heat the bacon fat in a large pot set over medium-high heat. Sauté the onion in the bacon fat, stirring often, until the edges begin to brown, about 5 minutes.

Add the ham hock, minced garlic, chicken stock and water and bring to a simmer. Cover and cook for 1 hour.

Add the collard greens to the pot and cook until tender, another 45 minutes to an hour.

Remove the ham hock, pull the meat off the bones and chop. Mix the meat back with the greens and serve.

Have vinegar and hot sauce at the table so guests can use at their preference.

These greens are a must to compliment any Southern dinner. Add Kentucky Spoon Bread and Southern Fried Chicken for a Sunday dinner to be requested often.

Grilled Mexican Corn

Prep time: 10 minutes

Cook time: 10 minutes

Serves : 8

Level: Easy

INGREDIENTS:

* 6 to 8 medium ears sweet corn, husks removed

* 1/2 cup Mexican crema, or sour cream

* 1/2 cup mayonnaise

* 1/2 cup minced cilantro

* 1 clove garlic, minced

* 1/4 teaspoon ground chipotle pepper, to taste

* 2 teaspoons lime zest, from one lime

* 2 tablespoon lime juice, from one lime

* 1/2 cup cotija cheese, crumbled

* Lime wedges, to serve

Directions:

Heat a gas or charcoal grill to 400 degrees. Clean the grates once it has

In a bowl, whisk together the crema, mayonnaise, cilantro, garlic, chipotle pepper, lime zest and lime juice. Taste and season the mixture with salt if needed. (Crema has a little salt already, so adjust to taste.) Set aside.

Grill the corn: Place the husked corn directly onto grill grates.

Grill the corn for about 3 minutes, undisturbed, or until kernels begin to turn golden brown and look charred. Turn over and repeat.

When all sides are browned, remove from the grill onto a platter.

Using a brush or a spoon, coat each ear of corn with the crema mixture. Sprinkle with crumbled cojita cheese.

Serve immediately with extra lime wedges.

For a really easy grilling occasion leave part of stock and husks attached while grilling keeping them moist as to not burn. Very festive way to serve directly from the fire. I've had these all over the Southwest

Pickled Beet Eggs

Prep: 10

Cook: 15 for hard boiled eggs

Inactive: 48 to 72 hours

Serves 10 to 12

Level: Easy

Ingredients:

* 3 (12 ounce) cans whole pickled beets

* 1 dozen shelled hard boiled eggs

* 1 cup water

* 1/2 cup apple cedar vinegar

Directions:

In a very large glass container place canned beets with the juice, apple cedar vinegar, water and eggs. Gently shack to mix well

Place in refrigerator for 48 to 72 hours . The longer you allow to set the better the taste becomes.

This egg side dish is another recipe I came across thanks to Grandmothers love of writing down every recipe from her Grandmother and Great Grandmother. She said it goes back to around 1800 from their farm in Michigan. I am not a real fan of plain hard boiled eggs or beets but I can finish off 6 of these at a time.

Green Bean Casserole

Prep: 5 minutes

Cook: 30

Serves: 8

Level: Easy

Ingredients:

* 2 cans (14.5 oz each) French-style green beans, drained

* 1 can (10.5 oz) condensed cream of mushroom soup

* 1/4 cup milk

* 1 container (2.8 oz) French-fried onions

Directions:

Preheat oven to 350°F.

In 1 1/2-quart casserole or glass baking dish, mix green beans, soup and milk.

Bake 20 to 25 minutes until bubbly, top with onions during last 5 minutes of baking.

Serve immediately.

This side dish should be served all year long as from experience most of my friends and family continually state that waiting for the holidays and green bean casserole makes their year end so wonderfully.

Cheesy Asparagus Gratin

Prep: 25 minutes

Cook: 10 to 12 minutes

Serves: 6 to 8

Level: Easy

Ingredients:

* 4 tablespoons (1/2 stick) unsalted butter, divided, plus more for baking dish

* 2 teaspoons kosher salt, divided, plus more for blanching water

* 2 pounds fresh asparagus, trimmed

* 1/2 teaspoon freshly-ground black pepper

* 2 tablespoons all-purpose flour

* 1/4 teaspoon cayenne pepper

* 1 1/2 cups whole milk

* 3 ounces Gruyere cheese, grated (about 3/4 cup)

* 3 ounces white cheddar cheese, grated (about 3/4 cup)

* 1 cup Panko (Japanese-style breadcrumbs)

Directions:

Preheat oven to 400 degrees with rack in highest position.

Butter a 3-quart baking dish.

Bring a large pot of salted water to a boil over high. Add half of the asparagus and cook until crisp-tender, 2 to 4 minutes (depending on thickness of spears). Remove with tongs, drain, and transfer to prepared dish. Repeat with remaining asparagus; toss with 1 teaspoon of the salt and 1/4 teaspoon of the black pepper.

Discard water; melt 2 tablespoons of the butter in same pot over medium-low. Whisk in flour and cayenne and cook, stirring constantly, until slightly darker in color, about 2 minutes. Slowly whisk in milk. Increase heat to medium, and simmer, whisking often, until thickened, about 5 minutes.

Add Gruyere, cheddar, 1/2 teaspoon of the salt, and remaining 1/4 teaspoon black pepper, and whisk until cheese is melted. Pour cheese sauce evenly over asparagus.

Melt remaining 2 tablespoons butter in a skillet over medium; stir in Panko and remaining 1/2 teaspoon salt. Scatter over asparagus.

Bake until warmed through, 8 to 10 minutes. Increase oven temperature to broil; broil until breadcrumbs are golden brown, 1 to 2 minutes.

This side dish can be served with your everyday dinners or featured at any fancy holiday meal. This dish is absolutely delicious.

Fried Sweet Corn

Prep: 15 minutes

Cook: 10 minutes

Serves: 4 to 6

Level: Easy

Ingredients:

* 6 to 8 ears fresh sweet corn cut from cob

* 1 stick sweet cream salted butter

* Sea salt

* Fresh cracked pepper

Directions:

In medium cast iron skillet melt butter on low heat. Add the corn and increase heat to medium high. Stirring constantly cook the corn until it begins to caramelize. About 10 minutes.

Salt and pepper to taste and serve immediately.

*Do not burn the butter during frying and you will have an amazing take on the every day corn dish. *

This recipe I found again after years of looking through the many recipes my Grandmother had stuffed in the hundreds of cook books in her library. Its funny because in all her years of cooking not once do I ever remember her having any one of those cook books any where near the kitchen while preparing a meal. The heading on the recipe said "fried sweet corn from Virginia plantation we visited in 1834". I presume from the date it was from my great-great grandmother .

Great Grandma's Brussels Sprouts

Prep: 15 minutes

Cook: 12 to 15 minutes

Serves: 6 to 8

Level: Easy

Ingredients:

* 2 pounds fresh Brussels sprouts

* Sea salt

* Fresh cracked pepper

* 1/4 cup water

* 1 stick sweet cream unsalted butter

* 1/4 cup good quality balsamic vinegar

Directions:

Cut sprouts in quarters and wash well

and place in large cast iron skillet with the water and steam sprouts for about 10 minutes.

Drain the water and reduce the heat to low. Melt the butter and return the

the sprouts and cook for about 5 to 6 minutes more.

Salt and pepper to taste and drizzle with balsamic vinegar just before serving.

Remember DO NOT over salt these as the vinegar will add saltiness too. This is an old recipe and with hope it will change your mind on whether or not you like this delicious vegetable.

Super Easy Roasted Vegetables

Prep: 15 minutes

Cook: 15 minutes

Serves: 6

Level: Easy

INGREDIENTS:

* 2 cup broccoli florets

* 2 cups white button mushrooms

* 1 zucchini, sliced and quartered

* 1 yellow squash, sliced and quartered

* 1 red bell pepper, chopped

* 1 yellow bell pepper, chopped

* 1 red onion, chopped

* 2 tablespoons olive oil

* 2 tablespoons balsamic vinegar

* 4 cloves garlic, minced

* 1 1/2 teaspoons dried thyme

* Kosher salt and

* Freshly ground black pepper

DIRECTIONS:

Preheat oven to 425 degrees .

Lightly oil a baking sheet or coat with nonstick spray.

Place broccoli florets, mushrooms, butternut squash, zucchini, squash, bell pepper and onion in a single layer onto the prepared baking sheet. Add olive oil, balsamic vinegar, garlic and thyme; season with salt and pepper, to taste.

Gently toss to combine.

Place into oven and bake for 12-15 minutes, or until tender.

I prefer this method of vegetable preparation to almost all others. It brings out the true taste of them that is lost when steaming or boiling in water. Add some garlic and pearl onions for an even more delicious side dish at your holiday table.

Dilly Green Beans

Prep: 5 minutes

Cook: 5 to minutes

Serves: 4 to 8

Level: Easy

Ingredients:

* 1 or 2 (8 ounce) cans cut green beans drained

* 1/2 stick real sweet cream salted butter

* 1 tablespoon dried dill weed

* 1 tablespoon dark soy sauce

Directions:

In medium sauce pan add green beans, butter and soy sauce. heat through over medium heat, tossing gently as to not break up beans.

Transfer to serving dish and sprinkle with the dried dill. and serve immediately.

The addition of the dill brings a light refreshing addition to the beans. Do not add salt as the soy sauce gives you all the saltiness needed in this dish. As a young boy this is the only way my Mother could get me anywhere near a canned green bean. try them on your family and see how easy it is to get them to eat all their veggies.

I hope in these pages you have come across a recipe or recipes that bring back memories of your own youth, Mother , Grandmother or special holiday celebration you thought you had all but forgotten. Keeping these old recipes alive for future generations to enjoy not only will create unforgettable dinners but memories of family and friends that will last a life time.

Just to remind everyone just as we dress ourselves for special dinners and occasions we too should dress our dinner tables. Whether it be as simple as fall leaves spread on a plain linen table cloth with colorful mismatched dishware or an elaborate center piece on Grandmothers finest lace using her finest china. The love you put forth will be noticed and forever treasured by all that attend. Cook with love for food and love of family and friends. You will never go wrong. Imagination, Love, Good food, family and friends equal unforgettable memories that will be held close to everyone's hearts for a life time.

Be adventurous try new things. The boxed dinners, drive up windows and new age way of "doing" dinner will still be there . Make the attempt to do a "home made" dinner offering tonight . The smiles you are sure to get in return will last in your memory and theirs a lot longer than "was it from a box , the freezer, or drive through window last night?"

Always Love and Good Cooking, Levi

Levi Vernon Springer IV

levispringerusa3@gmail.com

3002 Stadium Drive Apt D8

Phenix City Alabama 36867

254-278-9368

Made in the USA
Columbia, SC
10 October 2023